CAMBRIDGE SKILLS FOR FLUENCY
Series Editor: Adrian Doff

Speaking 1

Joanne Collie
Stephen Slater

CAMBRIDGE
UNIVERSITY PRESS

Anne-Marie Sykes
108 Cleveland Road
Ealing
London W13 0EL

PUBLISHED BY THE PRESS SYNDICATE OF THE UNIVERSITY OF CAMBRIDGE
The Pitt Building, Trumpington Street, Cambridge, United Kingdom

CAMBRIDGE UNIVERSITY PRESS
The Edinburgh Building, Cambridge CB2 2RU, UK
40 West 20th Street, New York, NY 10011–4211, USA
477 Williamstown Road, Port Melbourne, VIC 3207, Australia
Ruiz de Alarcón 13, 28014 Madrid, Spain
Dock House, The Waterfront, Cape Town 8001, South Africa

http://www.cambridge.org

First published 1991
Eleventh printing 2002

Printed in the United Kingdom at the University Press, Cambridge

ISBN 0 521 36788 3 Book
ISBN 0 521 36609 7 Cassette

Contents

Map of the book

Unit	Themes/Vocabulary areas	Areas of communication	Learner activities
1	Names, stage names, nicknames.	Talking about yourself and other people; asking about other people.	Recording information; guessing game; discussion; role play; group writing.
2	Appearance, personality; animals; age.	Describing people/personality; giving and receiving instructions.	Grid-filling; comparing choices; group writing; using instructions.
3	Colours, shades; shopping; class/town environment; letters; hospital; sickness.	Talking about likes, dislikes and intentions; making suggestions; persuading.	Vocabulary matching; discussion; completing questionnaires.
4	English in the classroom and outside; useful language for learners.	Negotiating choices; giving reasons; asking for explanations.	Comparing choices; discussion; completing questionnaires.
5	Keys; feelings and reactions; daily routine.	Describing objects and rooms; narrating experiences and sequences of events; making conjectures.	Exchanging anecdotes; interpreting a poem; guided fantasy; discussion.
6	Countries of the world and life in them; folk music.	Discussing hypothetical situations; exploring preferences; justifying opinions.	Labelling; exchanging information; comparing choices; guessing game.
7	Good/bad luck; lucky charms; lucky finds.	Talking about customs; predicting; relating personal experiences.	Discussion; listening and predicting; exchanging anecdotes; group project.
8	Fears/phobias; ways of overcoming fears/phobias.	Discussing emotions; making conjectures; giving advice.	Vocabulary matching; game; listening and discussion; reordering instructions.
9	Childhood games, toys, memories; personality traits.	Talking about the past; justifying opinions; agreeing/disagreeing; talking about behaviour.	Discussion; classifying vocabulary; guessing game; guided fantasy.

Unit	Themes/Vocabulary areas	Areas of communication	Learner activities
10	Food, ingredients, health aspects; restaurants.	Discussing likes/dislikes; persuading; planning future events.	Comparing reactions; role play; group planning; discussion; presenting ideas to the class.
11	Weather, forecasting; progress/difficulties with English.	Talking about hypothetical situations; using metaphor to describe people and feelings.	Gap-filling; completing a grid; listening and gap-filling; writing a poem; guessing game.
12	Families; personality, ability and appearance.	Describing personality; discussing relationships.	Discussion; making word drawings; interpreting a poem; group writing.
13	Public and private gardens; food for survival.	Describing an imagined scene; justifying opinions; negotiating choices.	Discussion; completing questionnaires; group planning; comparing choices.
14	Parties, festivals, celebrations, national days.	Talking about events, personal experiences and preferences.	Comparing choices; listening and guessing; group planning; role play.
15	Food recipes, recipes for success.	Getting information from written texts; exchanging information; expressing ideas metaphorically.	Reading and guessing; group writing game; comparing choices; listening and discussion.
16	Badges and tee-shirts; graffiti and dealing with it.	Talking about opinions; agreeing/disagreeing.	Group writing; comparing choices; discussion.
17	Litter and rubbish.	Exchanging views; negotiating choices; making conjectures; expressing likes/dislikes.	Completing a grid; listening and retelling; comparing choices; dialogue writing.
18	Air balloons; advertising.	Making conjectures; persuading.	Interpreting a picture; classifying vocabulary; listening; pair planning; drama presentation.
19	Lifestyles; home furnishings; simple pleasures; the quality of life.	Discussing likes/dislikes; agreeing/disagreeing; making conjectures.	Discussion; listening and discussion; completing a grid; comparing choices.
20	Assessment of this book.	Discussing feelings; justifying opinions; discussing progress or difficulties.	Comparing choices; exchanging views; group writing; self-assessment.

Acknowledgements

We should like to acknowledge the valuable help and support given by Adrian Doff and by Alison Baxter, Peter Donovan, Peter Ducker, Jeanne McCarten, Barbara Thomas and Angela Wilde of Cambridge University Press.

The authors and publishers would like to thank the teachers at the following institutions, where the material in *Speaking 1* was piloted, for all their constructive suggestions without which the improvements in the book would not have been made.
Australian College of English; British Council, Thessaloniki; British Institute, Madrid; British School of Genoa; Centre Malesherbes, Paris; English Language School, Crete; Footscray Adult Migrant Language Centre, Australia; INTERPERKS, Barcelona; ITC 'Sandro Boticelli', Rome; IUT Cergy, France; Klubschule Migros, Bern; Liceo Scientifico, Rome; Newnham Language Centre, Cambridge; Beatrice Schildknecht, Germany; South Australian Institute of Technology; Studio School of English, Cambridge; University of Queensland, Australia; VHS Hanover.

The authors and publishers are grateful to the following individuals and institutions for permission to reproduce copyright material:
Barnaby's Picture Library (pp. 2, 27 (top), 34); Christie's Fine Art Auctioneers (p. 5); Bibliothèque Nationale, Paris (p. 23); Sally and Richard Greenhill (p. 27 middle left and p. 52); Mickey Pallas (p. 29); the words of the song on p. 35 are from 'Raining in my Heart' (B&F Bryant) © Acuff Rose Opryland Music, Nashville, reproduced by permission of Acuff Rose Opryland Music Ltd, London and House of Bryant Publications, Tennessee; The Board of Trustees of the Royal Armouries (p. 36); *Portrait de Famille* 1954 by Dorothea de Tanning is © DACS 1990 (p. 38); the poem on p. 39 is called 'The Family' and is from *Pieces* by Robert Creeley, reprinted with permission of Charles Scribner's Sons, an imprint of Macmillan Publishing Company, copyright © 1969 by Robert Creeley; Harry Smith Horticultural Photographic Collection (p. 41); The Hutchison Library (p. 44); Home Office Crime Prevention (p. 50); Paddy Allen (p. 53); on p. 56 the poem is by Christopher Logue from 'Ode to the Dodo, Poems 1953–78' Turret Books and the poster is © Poems on the Underground, produced by students at the London College of Printing; p. 61 bottom right is courtesy of the Board of Trustees of the V&A; p. 61 top left is © Vincent van Gogh Foundation/National Museum Vincent van Gogh, Amsterdam; p. 61 top right *Trente* 1937 by Wassily Kandinsky is © ADAGP, Paris and DACS, London 1990; 'What a Wonderful World' by George David Weiss and Bob Thiele (p. 68) is © 1967 Range Road Music Inc. and Quartet Music Inc. All rights administered by Herald Square Music Inc. Used by permission. All rights reserved. Also by permission of Carlin Music Corporation, Ironbridge House, 3 Bridge Approach, Chalk Farm, London NW1 8BD.

The photographs on pp. 3, 12, 13, 16, 18, 20, 21, 22, 27 (2 photos bottom right), 30, 32, 43 and 54 were taken by Jeremy Pembrey. The photograph on p. 10 was taken by Nigel Luckhurst. The photographs on p. 55 were taken by Nicholas Collie.

Drawings by Chris Evans, David McKee and Pavely Arts. Artwork by Ace Art, Peter Ducker, Hardlines and Wenham Arts.

Book design by Peter Ducker MSTD.

1 | Sticks and stones may break my bones. . . .

Names and what they mean to us

MOOR

Frances and Henry thank Margaret, Tom and Peter for the wonderful party they gave us on Saturday, July 30, for our Golden Wedding. Also thanks to relatives and friends for the lovely presents and cards.

85773

ANNA and JOHN

Congratulations on the birth of our first grandson, James, born July 30. With all our love for a long and healthy life. Mum, Dad Kerry and Michael.

SOUTH FORD
Sarah and Robert

Congratulations on your recent engagement.

Wishing you both every happiness for the future.

Love Mum, Dad and all the family.

85781

WARD

Jane and David are delighted to announce the birth of their son, Benjamin Charles, born August 1, 8lb 2oz.

PITCHFORD
Steve and Kim

are delighted to announce the birth of their daughter, Carol Mary, born July 20. A little sister for Catherine.

84183

HELEN DIXON

Congratulations on your 18th birthday, August 4.

Love from Mum, Dad, Elizabeth and Jack.

84604

---

1 Tuning-in

Look at these family announcements from a newspaper. How many first names can you find in them?
With another student, write them down below. Add any other English names you know.
Do you know any English names which can be both a boy's name and a girl's name? Do you have names like that in your country?

Boys' names	Girls' names	Names for boys or girls
John	Anna	Kerry

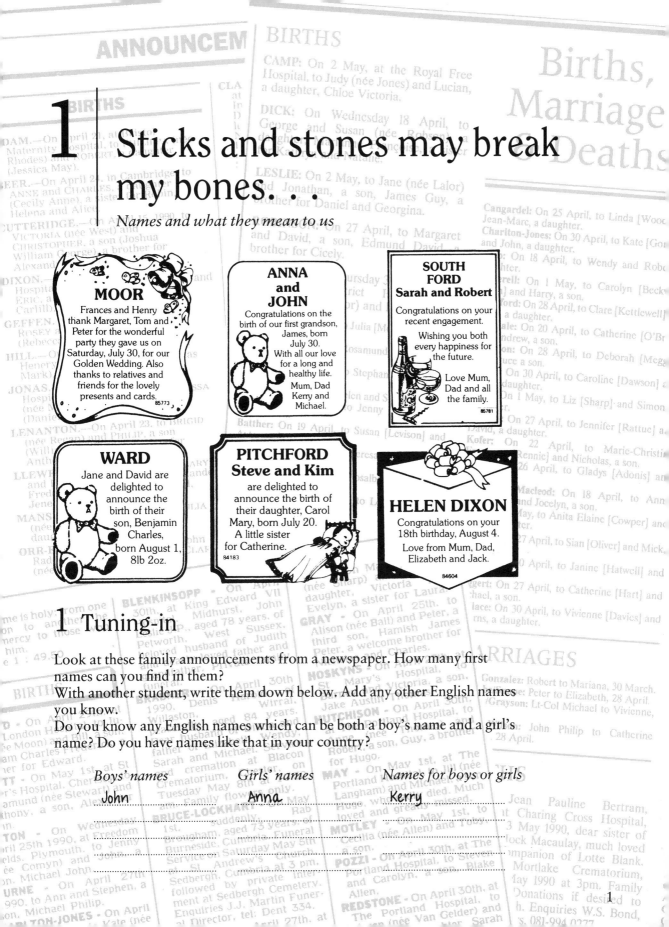

2 Is Rosita your dog?

Write down three first names that are important to you. They can be names of:

friends   family   people you do not like   animals   film stars
people in books   people in politics or sports   teachers

One student reads out the first name on his or her list. The others ask one question each. For example: 'Is Rosita your dog?' 'Is Rosita your mother?'
When the answer to your question is 'Yes', you get one point.
But if your very first question gets the answer 'Yes', you get two points.

3 The big apple and the dirty duck

The big apple. . .

Sometimes people give their houses a name. Here are some examples:

OAK TREE HOUSE

Maridon

(*Marion* and *Don*'s house)

SEA VIEW

BLISS COTTAGE

(Use your dictionary!)

Think of a good name for your house, flat or room.
With other students, talk about why you chose this name.
In your group, think of a new name for your school or college.

Cities can also have other names:

The Big Apple (New York)
The Mini Apple (Minneapolis)
Tinseltown (?)

With one other student, give your town or city a new name. Discuss it with the class. Can you all agree on a new name?

People sometimes change the names of pubs or hotels to make them funny.
For example:

The White Swan   becomes   *The Dirty Duck!*

Are there any funny names for hotels or shops in your town or city?
Talk about them with other students.

4 Names and more names

Ask another student these questions:

- Who chose your name?
- Did everyone in your family like the name?
- Is there another person in your family with the same name?
- Is there another first name you like better?

Actors or singers sometimes choose new names for the stage. Imagine you are going to become an actor *or* a singer. Think of a good name to help your career.

Now imagine the class is having a big party for actors and singers. Talk to the other guests. Introduce yourself: give your new name and say something about your plans for your career. Ask the others about their plans.

5 Nicknames

Some people have 'nicknames'. Nicknames tell you something about the person. What can you guess about these people?

Bomber Graham   Fingers MacBride   The Iron Lady
The Blonde Bombshell

Sometimes, nicknames are whole sentences that tell you something about the person. Here, for example, is a list of people in the same English class:

Carlos 'Sorry I'm late again' Delgado
Mohammed 'I need more grammar' Rashid
Martine 'I can't eat that' Bernadosse
Sayaka 'Have you marked my homework?' Harada
Maria 'I'm freezing' Bellini
Kurt 'Can we start now?' Schmidt
Juanita 'Hello everybody' Perez Borda
Azmi 'Can I borrow a pen please?' Abdullah

In groups, make up a sentence nickname for each person. Think of something that is interesting or special about that person. Write each nickname down. Don't put the real name with it. Give your list to another group and take theirs. Can you guess the name that goes with each nickname? How about a nickname for your teacher?

2 | Body shop
Our bodies

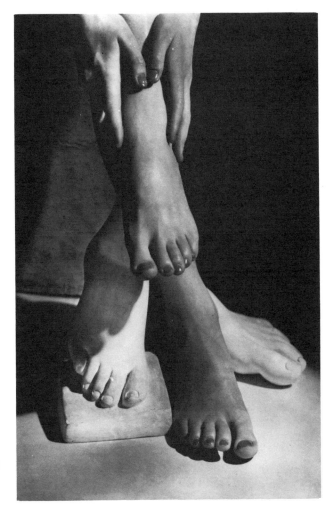

1 Tuning-in

Put a cross (✗) on each line to describe
yourself. Check the words first.
For example, if you think you are very
fit, put a cross like this:

fit —✗————————————— unfit

But if you are not very fit, put a cross like this:

fit —————————————✗— unfit

I AM:

fit —————————————	unfit
calm —————————————	nervous
hard-working —————————————	not hard-working

I HAVE:

a lot of energy —————————————	very little energy
a big appetite —————————————	a small appetite
quick reactions —————————————	slow reactions

Compare with another student. Did you put crosses in the same places? Talk
about the way you described yourself. Do you want to change? Why?

2 Body shop

Imagine you are in the future. Medical technology is very advanced. You can
now buy new parts for your body.
You have enough money to buy *two* new parts. Choose two from this list:

> *New parts*
> ears that hear thoughts
> joints that last for ever
> a heart that lasts 100 years
> skin that does not change
> hair that does not go grey or fall out
> legs that can walk as fast as a car
> X-ray eyes
> high-power muscles
> extra-strong hands

Find other students with the same choices as you. Talk about the reasons for
your choices:

> Why do you want these two new parts?
> How can they help you? How can they change your life?
> How are you going to use them?

3 Body insults

In English we sometimes make jokes – or funny insults – by comparing
people to animals.
With one or two other students, build up a list of joke insults. Take it in
turns, one by one. Use a dictionary to help you.

S/he has the brain of ....

.... the hair of ....

.... the face of ....

.... the charm of ....

.... the wisdom of ....

.... the energy of ....

.... the strength of ....

.... the politeness of ....

.... the appetite of ....

Here are some animals that you can use:

elephant   yak   cow   camel   dead rat   giraffe   ape
fox   toad   fly   hyena   rabbit   rhinoceros   spider
ostrich   goldfish   sparrow

4 Keep fit and relax

With another student, think up some simple exercises for the beginning of
your next English lesson. Here are some words and phrases to help you – but
you can use others.

Parts of the body	*Actions*		
eyes arm	breathe in	open	stretch out
mouth neck	breathe out	close	put
shoulder foot	turn bend		

Make up instructions for your exercises. Try your instructions out on
another group.

Now listen to the cassette. Can you do the exercises? Were your
instructions different from those on the cassette?

5 The perfect age

What is the perfect age for your mind and body? Write a number on each
line.

Body: 0 100
Mind: 0 100

Think of one reason for each choice. Tell another student your perfect ages,
and your reasons. Have you both chosen the same ages? Say why you think
your choices are better.

3 | Singing the blues

Colours

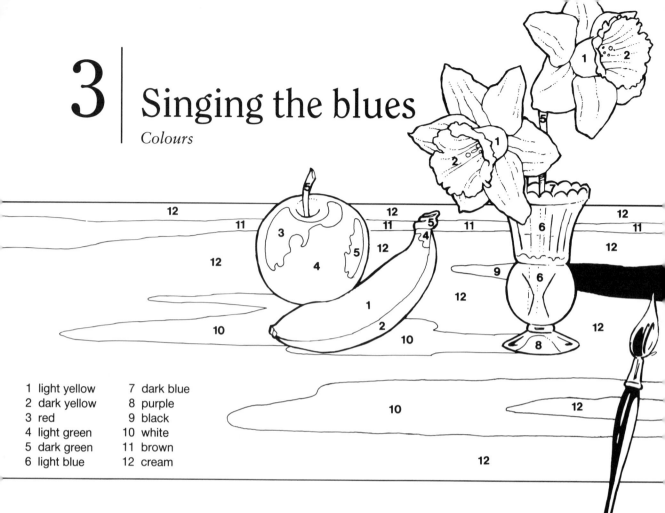

1 light yellow
2 dark yellow
3 red
4 light green
5 dark green
6 light blue

7 dark blue
8 purple
9 black
10 white
11 brown
12 cream

1 Tuning-in

Sometimes names of things are added to colours to show the exact shade.
Here is an example: 'lemon yellow' (the same shade as a lemon).
With another student, look at the names below and match them with one of
the three colours. If you don't know the words, ask another student or the
teacher.

RED	BLUE	GREEN

tomato   sky   apple   emerald   wine   olive   raspberry
navy   blood   sea   bottle   cornflower   cherry

Now think of a colour that you like. Can you find others in the class who
have chosen the same colour? With them, talk about your favourite shade of
that colour. For example, perhaps you like a light shade of yellow, but do not
like a darker mustard colour? Compare your ideas, and talk about some
things you have that are your favourite shade:

a bedspread   the walls of your bedroom   flowers   a painting
any other? ....

2 What colour shall we have?

Imagine you are going shopping. You can buy:

– one tee-shirt

– one pair of shoes

– one new car

Choose a colour for each thing. Write the colours down:

I'm going to buy a .... tee-shirt.
I'm going to buy a pair of .... shoes.
I'm going to buy a .... car.

Ask questions to find out what colours the others have chosen, and why.
Have they chosen their favourite colours?

3 Let's paint the town . . . and the classroom!

Look at the walls and the ceiling in your classroom. With another student,
talk about some new colours for the room. What colours are best for
learning English? Why?
As a class, vote for the colours you want. Remember the ceiling!

Now think of your town or city. Is there one street or one public building
that needs a new coat of paint? Decide on a colour, then see if others agree
with your choice.

In your town, is there a wall where you could paint a picture? Do you like
public buildings that have pictures on them? Are there any in your country?
Compare your ideas and talk about them with others in the class.

4 A colourful love letter

Imagine you are going to send a letter to your love.
With another student, choose a colour for the writing paper:

white	light green
cream	light blue
lemon yellow	light grey
orange	bright red
pink	wine red
lavender	

Now choose a colour for the ink:

green	brown
blue	turquoise
black	silver
red	gold

Together, write the first line of your love letter.

Try the same activity with these letters:
– a letter to a relative after someone in the family has died
– a letter to your teacher
– a thank-you letter to a friend who has given you a lovely present

5 Colour therapy

Imagine that the classroom is a small hospital with six rooms. Each room is a different colour. There is:

a red room
a pink room
a light blue room
a yellow room
a bright green room
a white room

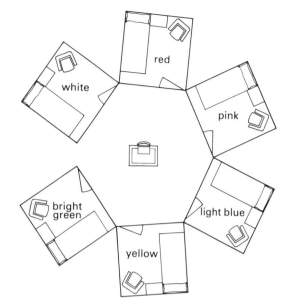

There are three patients arriving today:
– a young man with very bad depression
– a young woman who is going to have a baby
– an older man with heart problems

Role play With another student, each choose one of the following roles:

Student A: You are a doctor at the small hospital. Find out what the patient's problem is, then decide on the best room. Tell the patient why the colour of the room is best.

Student B: You are one of the three patients arriving at the hospital. Decide which room is best for you. Tell the doctor about yourself, and ask for the room you want.

6 What a wonderful world

Listen to the song on the cassette. Here is what one learner wrote about it. With another student, can you fill in the missing words and finish the last sentence?

The singer loves the world because it has so much colour. .... are green, ... are red, the .... is blue and .... are white. The colours make him feel happy and full of love. I feel like this when ....

....

4 | I didn't quite catch what you said

English in the classroom

1 Tuning-in

You are helping to write a book for learners of English. It has a unit called 'Phrases for the classroom'.

Which *six* phrases are the most useful? You can choose six from the list below, or think of other ones that you find useful.

What does . . . mean?
How do you spell . . . ?
Would you explain the differences between . . . and . . ., please?
Is there any homework this week?
What page are we on?
I'm sorry, I can't see the board.
Would you speak more slowly, please?
Would you go over that again, please?
Would you repeat that, please?
I didn't quite catch what you said.
See you next week/tomorrow/later.
Why are we doing this?
I've finished this, what do I do now?
How do you say . . . in English?
Would you write that on the board, please?

Compare choices. Can the class agree on a list of six phrases?

2 English in the classroom

Are there any English words on the walls of your classroom?
What else can you put on the walls? In small groups, decide which of these you can add:
- short poems in English
- words of songs in English
- posters or pictures with English on them
- a 'thought for the day'
- an advertisement (add a few words in English)
- an interesting headline (ask your teacher to help you translate one from your own newspapers, if you do not have English newspapers)
- your week's timetable in English (fill in the blanks in English – ask for help if you need it):

Monday	Tuesday	Wednesday	Thursday	Friday
a.m.				
p.m.				

See how many of these each group can find to put up! Is there anyone who doesn't want to put anything up?

3 English only?

A. It is a good idea to speak *only* English in English lessons.

B. It is *not* a good idea to speak *only* English in English lessons.

With another student, choose one sentence only, A or B, and try to think of at least two reasons for your choice. You can use some of the words and expressions below if you wish. You can also ask your teacher to help you. Now find one or two students who did not choose the same sentence as you. Tell them your reasons and listen to theirs.

We are here to learn English, after all.
Our English is not good enough yet.
You have to speak English to learn it.
We can't understand instructions in English.
The more English you hear, the better you can speak it.
I want to know what to do.
It's important to hear as much English as possible.
We are not children, after all.
I want to spend all my time in class listening to English.
I want to understand everything.
I want to learn English as fast as possible.
I need to say difficult things.
It's best to go slowly and make sure you understand everything.

4 I wish I could say . . .

In your own language write down two things you wish you could say in English.

Classes with the same first language
Put the sentences in a pile. In small groups, choose a few and try to put them into English. Your teacher will help you.

Classes with different first languages
Write one of your two sentences on the board, in turn. Other students and the teacher will guess what your sentence means and help you put it into English.

5 Questionnaire: English outside the classroom

Use either Questionnaire A or Questionnaire B. Find two other students, and ask them your questions.

English outside the classroom: Questionnaire A

```
1 Do you know any people outside the classroom who speak English?
2 Who are they?
3 Do you speak English with them?
   [ ]  If yes, what do you speak about?
   [ ]  If no, why not?   Too difficult
                          Embarrassing

                          . . . . . . . . . . . . . . . . . . . . . . . .

                          . . . . . . . . . . . . . . . . . . . . . . . .
4 Do you read anything in English outside the classroom?
   [ ]  If yes, what do you read? Where? How often?
   [ ]  If no, why not?   Too difficult
                          Not easy to find

                          . . . . . . . . . . . . . . . . . . . . . . .

                          . . . . . . . . . . . . . . . . . . . . . . .
```

English outside the classroom: Questionnaire B

```
1 Do you listen to English outside the classroom?
   [ ]  If yes,     where?
                    what do you listen to?
                    how often?
   [ ]  If no, why not?    Nothing to listen to
                          Don't feel like it

                          . . . . . . . . . . . . . . . . . . . . . . . .

                          . . . . . . . . . . . . . . . . . . . . . . . .
2 Do you ever write in English outside the classroom?
   [ ]  If yes,     what do you write?
                    how often?
   [ ]  If no, why not?    Too difficult
                          No one to write to

                          . . . . . . . . . . . . . . . . . . . . . . . .

                          . . . . . . . . . . . . . . . . . . . . . . . .
```

Talk about your answers. How can you use English more often outside the classroom? Share your ideas with other people in your class.

5 | Opening doors

Keys and what they unlock

1 Tuning-in

Put any keys from your pockets on the table.
Pick up a key (not your own) and talk about it. You can use these words to
help you:

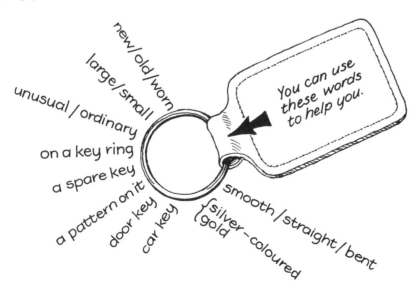

new/old/worn
large/small
unusual / ordinary
on a key ring
a spare key
a pattern on it
door key
car key
silver - coloured
gold
smooth / straight / bent

You can use these words to help you.

Then pick up your own keys again. Tell the other students what they open.
Ask one or two questions about their keys.

2 Where did I leave my keys?

Nearly everyone has a 'key' story – about losing keys, or about forgetting where they are. Sometimes people lock themselves out – or in!

Ask your teacher to tell you one of her/his key stories. Then listen to the cassette. What did your teacher and the person on the cassette feel about their key stories? Did they have happy endings?

Now, in groups, tell your own key stories. You can use these questions to help you tell your story:
– When did your key story happen?
– Where were you?
– Were you alone or with someone?
– How did you feel: annoyed?   angry?   sad?   panic-stricken?
– What happened in the end?

3 The key

Read this poem:

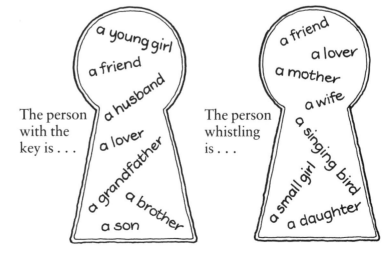

turn the key:
unexpected brightness, when
somewhere in the house
her whistle

Look at the people in each keyhole. Now read the poem again.
Who has the key?
Who is whistling?
Talk about your answers with another student; discuss any differences in the way you understand the poem.

The person with the key is . . .
a young girl
a friend
a husband
a lover
a grandfather
a brother
a son

The person whistling is . . .
a friend
a lover
a mother
a wife
a singing bird
a small girl
a daughter

4 I turn the key

Imagine that you are going home as you do each day. You arrive at the front door, and you put your key in the lock.
Tell your partner what you do, step by step. Start by saying: 'I turn the key . . . then I . . . then I . . .'

Now imagine that you have a magic key. When you turn the key in the lock, you can make a wish. You can wish for anything or anyone to be in the house when you open the door. You are going to find 'unexpected brightness'.

Take a few minutes to think about your wish before you turn the key. When you are ready, turn the key, go into the house, and say what happens this time, and how you feel.

Now listen to the cassette – were your wishes like those on the cassette?

5 Through the keyhole

Who is she? Where is she? Why is she there? What can she see through the keyhole?
With another student, prepare answers to these questions and be ready to talk to other pairs about them.

6 | It's a small world

Foreign countries – travel

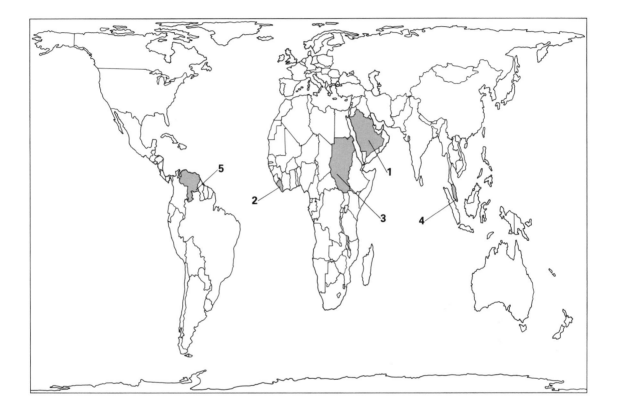

1 Tuning-in

Look at the map of the world with another student. Talk about the countries
which are numbered. Can you name them?
Choose the correct countries from this list:

Malaysia   Hong Kong   Kenya   South Korea   Egypt
Nigeria   Sudan   Peru   Iran   Venezuela   Cameroon
Saudi Arabia   Liberia

2 Where are they now?

Do any of your friends or relatives live in other countries? On your map, mark 'F' for friends and 'R' for relatives to show where they are.

Exchange maps with another student. Ask questions to find out about their friends and relatives.

Compare maps with other students in the class. Do two people in your class have friends or relatives in the same part of another country?

Where do your teacher's friends and relatives live?

3 A new life in a different country

Imagine that you have to move from your country. Where could you live happily for the rest of your life?

I'd miss....

house/flat
flowers   smells   family
cinema   theatre   people
shops   restaurants   friends   food

Choose three countries and explain your choices to one or two other students. Have you got the same opinions?

What things from your homeland would you miss most?

Now listen to the cassette, and compare your choices with those of the speaker. Would you miss some of the same things?

20

4 International Folk Music Festival

 Listen to these short pieces of folk music from different countries. With another student, try to guess where each piece comes from.

Talk about your guesses. Have other students chosen the same countries?

Do you have any records or tapes of music from different countries? Talk about one or two singers or musicians that you like from other countries.

5 The three most . . .??? countries in the world

With another student choose two of the boxes below. Together write your two lists of countries. Talk about reasons for your choices.

Now, in small groups, read out your lists of countries. Can others guess which box each list belongs to? Say why you agree or disagree with other people's lists.

In the whole world, which countries are:

the three most mysterious?

the three healthiest?

the three most dangerous?

the three most dynamic?

the three most sophisticated?

the three most unstable?

the three most inefficient?

the three most beautiful?

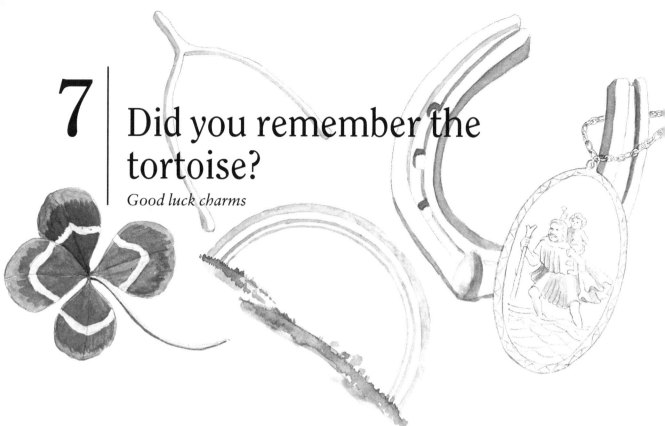

7 | Did you remember the tortoise?

Good luck charms

1 Tuning-in

What are the things in the picture above? Why do people keep them? Think about other things people have, in your country, for the same reason. Describe them.

2 Black cat

Some people think a black cat brings bad luck. Some people think it brings good luck.
Read this list and with another student guess which ones bring bad luck and which ones bring good luck.

salt
a golden butterfly
the first star in the evening
a line in the pavement
saying 'Break a leg' to an actor
a glass smashed in the fireplace
a broken mirror

Are there other things which bring bad luck in your country?

22

3 A stroke of luck in Sweden

Listen to the story on the cassette. Can you guess the ending?

Now think of a time when you or someone you know were very lucky. With one or two other students, tell the story up to the point just *before* the lucky ending. Can the others in your group guess what happened?

4 A lucky find

In Ballarat in Australia people still find pieces of pure gold near the old mines.
Have you ever found any of the things below? Which ones? Where did you find them? What did you do with them?

> money or a wallet   a ring   a watch   a pen   a knife
> a photograph   clothing   a fossil   a passport
> something else: ....

Talk about your lucky finds with a few other students.

Now listen to the cassette – what do you think of these lucky finds?

5 Chinese tortoise

The tortoise is a lucky animal in China. With some other students, decide on a good luck animal for your English class.

Then tell the class what animal you have chosen and why.

Make a simple design to put up in your classroom. What good luck do you want your animal to bring? Don't forget to take it with you to your next English exam! Good luck!

8 | The mad professor

Fears and phobias

1 Tuning-in

Can you match these names with the creatures in the picture? Don't look at your dictionary. Ask other students to help you.

bat   rat   crab   mosquito   snake   frog   spider

With another student, look at the creatures you have named. Answer the question in the box by putting names in three lists. Do you all agree?

> Which creatures have:

sharp teeth   tails   poison

....

....

2 The mad professor's experiment

You are helping Professor Greymatter with his experiment on fear.
Imagine that you are holding out your hand. The teacher will call out the
names of *four* creatures. As the teacher calls out each one, imagine that you
have it on your hand.

Write down the name of each creature and a number between 1 and 10 that
shows your fear of that creature.

(NO FEAR AT ALL) 1 . . . 2 . . . 3 . . . 4 . . . 5 . . . 6 . . . 7 . . . 8 . . . 9 . . . 10 (TOTAL PANIC)

After the experiment, count up your total. Don't show it to anyone.

Now, with one or two other students, try to guess:
– Which person in the class has the lowest total?
– Which person in the class has the highest total?
– What is your teacher's total score?

3 I'm frightened of . . .

People are frightened of many different things:

flying   heights   the dark   exams   water
making mistakes in English   the boss   very small places
very open places   dying   going mad
walking alone at night in a big city

▶ Listen to the cassette. What are they frightened of?

Person 1	
Person 2	
Person 3	

Talk about your answers with other students.

▶ Now listen to another group of people on the cassette. What *three*
things are they frightened of?

Are you frightened of the same things? Ask other students. Can you say why
you are frightened?
What about your friends and family? What are they frightened of?
Do you know anyone who is not frightened of *anything*?

4 You don't have to be afraid

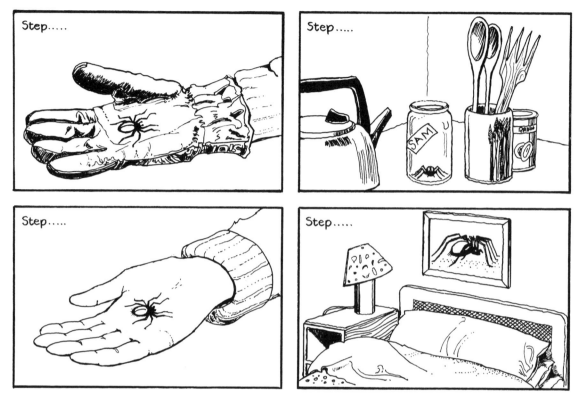

Here are four steps to help someone who is frightened of spiders but they are not in the right order. This is the instruction for Step 1:

STEP 1: PUT A PICTURE OF A SPIDER ON YOUR BEDROOM WALL.

With another student put the four steps in the right order and talk about the instructions for the other three steps. See if other students have the same order and the same instructions. Can you think of Step 5?

[cassette icon] Listen to the cassette. What instructions are there for helping people who are frightened of crowds? Do you agree? Talk about it with others in the class.

With one or two students, think of a few steps to help people who are frightened of one of these things:

swimming   taking exams   being alone in the dark
speaking English

Share your ideas with other groups and with the teacher.

9 | Once a child, always a child?

Memories of childhood

1 Tuning-in

When you were a child, what were your favourite games, toys or pastimes?

Where did you play the games?
How often?
Did you play with other people?
Who?
How old were you?

2 When does someone stop being a child?

Choose one answer from this list or write your own.

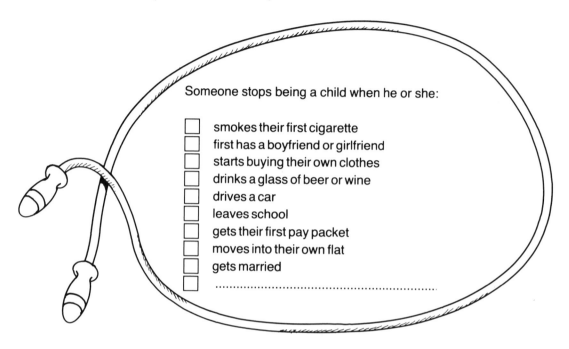

Someone stops being a child when he or she:

☐ smokes their first cigarette
☐ first has a boyfriend or girlfriend
☐ starts buying their own clothes
☐ drinks a glass of beer or wine
☐ drives a car
☐ leaves school
☐ gets their first pay packet
☐ moves into their own flat
☐ gets married
☐ ....

Find others in the class with the same answer as you. Talk about why you chose it.

How old were you when you stopped being a child – or are you still a child in some ways? Tell another student your ideas. What about your teacher?

3 Nobody's perfick . . .

What are children like? Here are some words to help you talk about them. With another student, look at these words. Do you know some of them? Can you guess what the others mean? If not, look in a dictionary or ask the teacher.

shy noisy spoilt cheerful stubborn cheeky
curious active lazy obedient quiet
easy-going untidy lonely tidy
friendly mischievous serious

Now put the words in one of these three lists:

Parents like a child who is:	Parents don't want their child to be:	Parents aren't sure about a child who is:
....	....	....
....	....	....
....	....	....
....	....	....
....	....	

Compare with other students. Do you all agree?

4 Nobody's perfick . . . except me

Were you a . . . good child? . . . a naughty child? . . . a quiet child? What sort of child were you?

On a piece of paper, write down three words that describe the sort of child you were. When you are ready, give your paper to the teacher.
Guess which word your class has used most often. Write it down.

Ask two students to read out all the words on the papers. Each time you hear a word, put a cross next to it on the list. At the end, count the number of crosses. Which word has most crosses?

Think about your own three words again. Can you use the same words to describe yourself today? Talk about this with another student.

5 The missing photo

Think of a special day in your childhood – but a day when nobody took a photo. Imagine you can go back to that day and take a photo. Listen to some instructions.

With another student, talk about your photo. Remember to talk about the day, the place, the people, the clothes, and the things you are doing in the photo. Ask your teacher about his or her photo.

10 | Try one of these
Food

1 Tuning-in

With some other students, guess what has gone into these sausages. Look at the list of ingredients and choose the ingredients that you think are in the sausages:

meat   spices   rice   bread   preserving agents   acids
onions   water   mustard   potatoes   salt   butter

Would you like to try these sausages? Can you say why? What about other students? Do you have sausages or something like a sausage in your country? What is in them?

2 Try one of these . . .

Imagine that everyone in the class is in a supermarket. Choose one of these
roles:

Your company makes sausages. You have a plate of sausages. Ask people to try one.

You are shopping in the supermarket. Some people want you to try one of their sausages. You can say yes or no, and say what you think of the sausage.

3 A meal in a jacket

Many countries have 'pies' – food inside a 'jacket', so that it is easier to eat.
With another student, plan an interesting pie – made with anything good to
eat.
When you have planned the ingredients, draw a picture of the new pie. List
the ingredients beside the picture.

Now decide:
– Which shops in your town will sell the new pie?
– When is it best to eat it – what meal of the day?
– What is nice to drink with it?
– What other food goes well with it?

Food fair: There is a food fair this week in your town. Tell people about your
new pie and the healthy things in it.

4 Is good food irresistible?

With one or two other students, write different foods in lists under the four headings.
You can write the same food in more than one list. Discuss the meaning of the headings first.

Good food	Disgusting food	Dangerous food	Irresistible food
....	....	....	....
....	....	....	....
....	....	....	....
....	....	....	....

Can your class agree?
How do you know which food is dangerous?
How do you avoid dangerous food?

5 Opening your first restaurant

You and another student are going to open a new restaurant in your town or city. Together, decide on these things. Then tell the class about your new restaurant.

1 What are you going to call it?
2 Where in the town is it going to be?
3 What opening hours are you going to have?
4 What style of food are you going to offer?
5 What will your restaurant look like:
   – What colour rooms?
   – What style of furniture?
   – What kind of lighting?
   – What pictures on the walls?
6 What special features are you going to have:
   – live music?
   – candles?
   – open cooking fires?
   – any others?

11 | It's raining in my heart
The weather

1 Tuning-in

Here are some weather symbols from a newspaper. With another student, put in the missing words next to the right symbols.

Missing words:

Sleet
Fine-weather clouds
Rain and sunny intervals
Thunder and lightning
Dull-weather clouds

What kind of weather do you like best? Talk about it with your partner.

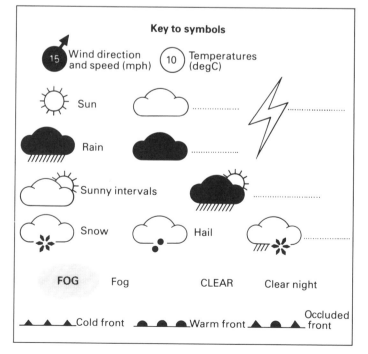

Key to symbols

15 Wind direction and speed (mph)   10 Temperatures (degC)

Sun

Rain

Sunny intervals

Snow   Hail

FOG Fog   CLEAR Clear night

Cold front   Warm front   Occluded front

2 The perfect day

Imagine you can make weather exactly as you want it. With another student, plan one day of perfect weather for next week. Write your weather for that day in the boxes.

	Temperature	Hours of sunshine	Light winds / heavy winds / gales	Light rain / heavy rain / storms	Light snow / heavy snow / blizzards
Monday					
Tuesday					
Wednesday					
Thursday					
Friday					
Saturday					
Sunday					

Describe your perfect day to another pair. Ask questions about their day.
What are they going to do on that day?
With the rest of the class build up the weather for a perfect week.

3 It's raining in my heart

Listen to the song. Put in the missing words, then compare your answer with another student's.

The sun is out
The sky is ....
There's not a ....
To .... the view
But it's raining
Raining in my heart.

The weatherman
Says .... today
He doesn't know
That you've ....
And it's raining
Raining in my heart.

Oh, oh misery, oh misery
Oh, what's going to become of me?

⟫→

Now write a short poem: use a weather word to say what your feelings are.

This is our poem:

> My world is full of sunshine
> Because I am with you.

When you have written your poem, take turns saying it to other students.

4 Six sunny intervals

Weather announcers use some of these phrases when they give a weather forecast for the next day:

chance of heavy rain   rain turning to sleet
fog patches clearing slowly   sunny and dry all day
chance of a thunderstorm   occasional showers
possibility of heavy snow   variable winds
light to moderate winds   gale warnings
temperatures above average   changeable weather

Can you think of any others?

Here is a weather description of Henry VIII, a famous English king:

Above average temperatures, but changeable. Variable wind directions. Frequent gales and thunderstorms. Six sunny intervals.

With another student, choose a famous person from your country or another country, past or present. Together, decide on a weather description for that person.

Can other pairs guess who it is?

5 Fog patches clearing slowly

Tell other students about your progress in English. Use some of the weather expressions to complete the three sentences below:
- When I first started learning English . . .
- This week . . .
- Next year . . .

12 | Five ways

Families

1 Tuning-in

With another student, talk about this picture. What is the artist suggesting about the people and the dog in this family?

Here are some words that may be useful. You can use a dictionary or ask your teacher for help if you need to.

strong   weak   dominant   dependent   submissive   cold
harsh   passive   sad   soft   important/unimportant

2 Word drawings of families

Here are diagrams drawn by three people to show
their families. Can you say what each drawing
suggests about that person's family?
Talk about them with one or two other students.

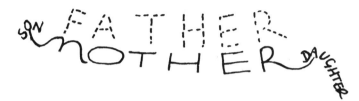

3 My word drawing

On a piece of paper, make your own word drawing.
It can be a word drawing of: your family
                               your friends
                               your English class

When you are ready, exchange your word drawing with another person.
Talk about your partner's drawing. Ask questions about it.

4 Five ways

Father
and mother
and sister
and sister
and sister

    *

Here we are
There are five
ways to say this

Robert Creeley

How many people are there in the poem?
Who is speaking in the poem? Is it the father?
What are the 'five ways' to say this?

Think about your answers to these questions, then discuss your ideas with
other students.

5 A new arrival in the family

'. . . and the princess had for godmothers all the Fairies they could find in the kingdom (of who.n they found seven) that every one of them might give her a gift.'
from *Sleeping Beauty*

Imagine there is a new baby in your family. You have the power to give the baby seven gifts, but not ordinary gifts: gifts of character or ability or appearance, from people you know or famous people.

With a few other students, decide on your seven gifts. An example has been written in for you.

Our seven gifts:

1 Leonardo da Vinci   's imagination

2 .... 's ....

3 .... 's ....

4 .... 's ....

5 .... 's ....

6 .... 's ....

7 .... 's ....

13 | A tulip for friendship

Gardens – plants

1 Tuning-in

Here is a garden wall. Imagine what is behind it. You can use some of these words to help you if you like.

enclosed formal wild

flowers fountains

birds fish ponds

streams bridges

waterfalls seats

paths statues

lawns fruit trees

stepping stones

Describe the garden behind the wall to another student.
Choose a book to read in the garden – where is the best spot to sit when you are reading by yourself?
Choose a good spot to sit and have a chat with a friend.
Now tell your partner about the book you have chosen, and the best spot to read or to chat.

2 Public gardens

Take this questionnaire with you when class is finished. Ask two people who are not in your class the questions on it.

---

1. In our town we need new public gardens   YES/NO

2. If the answer is YES:

    The best place for new public gardens is ....

    In our new public gardens we need: (tick three)

    [ ]   a playground for children

    [ ]   a zoo

    [ ]   lots of flowers

    [ ]   grass with chairs for people to sit in the sun

    [ ]   a special picnic place

    [ ]   a place where people can cook outdoors

    [ ]   a swimming pool

    [ ]   a paddling pool for children

    [ ]   lots of fountains

    [ ]   other things? ....

3. If the answer is NO:

    What is more important than new public gardens?

    Can we improve the public gardens we have? How?

Bring the questionnaire with you to the next English class. Report your answers to the class. What ideas are the most popular?

3 A garden for our English class

Are there any plants in your classroom? Do you and other students in your class think it is a good idea to have plants in the classroom?

Think of one reason why it *is* – or *isn't* – a good idea to have plants in the English classroom. When each of you is ready, give your reason to the class.

As a class, decide which reason was: the most interesting . . .

the funniest . . .

4 A food garden

Imagine you are starting a new life on a very small island. It is beautiful but rocky. It has the same climate as your country. There is only one place where you can make a garden to grow food.

You can carry with you five plants to put in your food garden. With three other students, decide what plants you will grow in your garden.

Tell the class about your five plants. Give reasons for your choices.

Now listen to the cassette. Were your choices the same? Talk about the differences, if any.

5 A tulip for friendship

Imagine you are going to plant a window-box for your English classroom. Each student can choose one plant or flower, with a special meaning. For example:
   a tulip for friendship
   a cactus for difficulties with English
   a palm tree for sunny days
   ....

Think about your plant or flower. If you need help, ask the teacher or use a dictionary. When you are ready, write your plant on the board, with its meaning.

When everyone has written a plant or flower, decide, with another student, which of those plants you want to put in your window-box. Ask other pairs about their window-boxes.

14 | Let's have a party
Celebrations

1 Tuning-in

What do you celebrate? Choose as many of the following as you like, and add more of your own. Talk about your answers with another student.

religious festivals   national day   weddings   divorces
births   winning at sports   winning an election   passing an exam
getting a new job   getting a promotion   retiring
Friday or Saturday – end of the week's work

2 Let's have a party

🔊 Listen to the cassette. Guess what the four people are celebrating. Here are some possible answers:

a lucky escape   getting a new job   paying a debt   a divorce
a marriage   moving to a new house

Person 1	
Person 2	
Person 3	
Person 4	

With another student, talk about your last birthday. How did you celebrate?

3 International Children's Day

With a few other students, plan a new international day for children.

1 Choose *one* of these themes for the day:

> PEACE   HEALTH   EDUCATION   FAMILY LIFE

2 Choose a date.

3 Now plan celebrations in your town for that date. Decide on:
  - where to have the celebrations
  - a famous person to start the celebrations
  - food and drink for the children
  - games or other activities for the children
  - music

Describe your celebration plans to the class.

4 Let's celebrate today

What can you celebrate today? Think of a reason for a celebration.

Write your reason on a piece of paper.

Collect all the answers and read them out. Are any the same? Decide as a class which one you like best.

5 Party guests

You have now decided on a reason to celebrate today. Imagine that you are going to have a party. You can invite famous people of the present or the past. They can be real people or people from books or films.

Choose one famous person. Then, sitting in small groups, tell each other the person you want to invite. Together, decide on two of the famous people. Now write them on the board. This is your guest list.

As a class, think up a different question to ask each guest.

Choose one of the guests from the list. Imagine you are that famous person. What is your answer to the question?

15 | Ten mouthfuls of conversation

Cooking and recipes

1 Tuning-in

Here are some recipes. With another student, try to guess what each recipe is
for. Use a dictionary if you wish.

3 cups flour.
2 tablespoons butter.
1½ cup mashed potato.
¼ cup milk.
pinch of salt.

Mix all the ingredients.
Make a paste.
Roll it out on a board.
Cut into rounds.
Bake in a hot oven.

1 pound of flour
2 tablespoons of vegetable oil
½ cup of salt
1 teaspoon red food colouring
1 teaspoon blue food colouring

Mix the oil, flour and salt together.
Make a paste. Add red colouring to one
half, blue colouring to the other half.
Leave for an hour under a wet cloth
before using.

1 large cupful of mustard
1 tablespoonful of salt
1 teaspoon pepper
½ cup boiling water
Mix everything together.
Make a thick paste.
Put the paste on to a clean
cloth and use while hot.

1 egg.
onion peel.
A few grains of rice.
An old nylon sock.

Place the egg, the peel and
the rice in the nylon sock.
Make sure the egg is in the middle.
Tie the sock.
Put it into boiling water for ten
minutes.

2 Measure for measure

Here is a recipe for cucumbers filled with rice, but all the measures and the ingredients are mixed up. With another student, try to put the right measures with the right ingredients.

rice
eggs
onion
butter
chicken
mushrooms
cucumbers
salt and pepper

4 slices 2 125 grams
1 pinch 50 grams
½ Cup 1 Large 3

3 A class recipe for a tasty dish

In groups of five: each person writes one ingredient on a piece of paper. Fold your paper and pass it to the student on your right. Now each person writes a new ingredient on the folded paper. Continue for five turns.

Each person now takes one recipe. Unfold your paper and read the recipe. Think of an exciting name for your new dish and decide how to cook or prepare it.

In pairs: invite your partner to dinner at your house. Tell him or her about your tasty new dish.

4 Recipe for success

Here is a recipe that is a bit different. Read it with another student. Ask the teacher for help if you need any.

To be a success in life you need:

20 kilos of luck

15 kilos of help from your family

5 years of education

10 mouthfuls of conversation

1 pinch of talent

1 new idea

3 kilos of energy

2 rich friends

Mix all the ingredients together and leave for several years.

With your partner, talk about what you need to be a success in life.
Choose the *three* most important ingredients from the recipe.
Choose the *three* least important.

Are there any ingredients missing from the recipe? Can you think of a better one? Compare your ideas with those of other groups.

5 My recipe for . . .

Listen to the cassette. The speaker is giving his recipe for a long and happy life. What do you think of his ideas? Compare your ideas with those of other students.

Now, with one or two students, decide on a recipe for:

A GOOD ENGLISH CLASS

You can use some of these ingredients if you like – but don't forget to say how much of each you need!

When you are ready, tell another group your recipe.

fun
a short period of time
music
mouthfuls of conversation
listening
books pictures cassettes
reading pretty or handsome video teacher
English speakers walking or dancing
friends colour different things to do
writing films
some time outside the classroom
games quiet times
interesting topics small groups
questionnaires singing

16 | The writing's on the wall
Graffiti

1 Tuning-in

With some other students, think of all the ways we can wear words:

    badges   labels on clothes   washing instructions on clothes

What other ways can you think of?

How many words are you wearing?

Write down the words each person is wearing in your group. Try to remember or guess the words you can't see!

Which group in the class has the most words?

2 Badges and tee-shirts

Work with a partner. Make up a phrase to put on a badge.
Use some of these words. Ask other people in your class
questions about their badges.

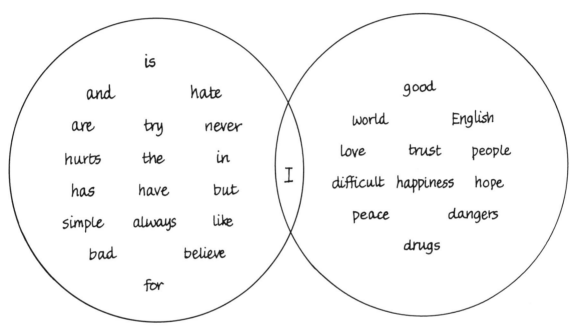

3 The writing's on the wall

In groups, put each piece
of graffiti into a suitable
category:

POLITICAL
FUNNY
PERSONAL
SILLY
POETIC

Compare and discuss
your results with another
group.

WE WANT
WORK

END VIOLENCE
TO WOMEN
TO NOW!.

make love not war
— i'm married, I do both PAT

BAN THE
BOMB

ROSES ARE RED, VIOLETS
ARE BLUE, WHY CAN'T BLACK
BE BEAUTIFUL TOO?

MICKEY MOUSE
IS A RAT

JOHN Geography is
Everywhere

ONCE I COULD NEVER
FINISH ANYTHING BUT NOW I...

IN 1788 THE ABORIGINES DISCOVERED CAPTAIN COOK

TOURISTS
YES
TROOPS
NO

4 What sort of people write graffiti?

Put a tick (✓) in column 1 to show what you think. Now ask at least one other person. Put a tick in column 2 to show what she or he thinks.

Most graffiti writers are:	1	2
young		
middle-aged		
old		
men		
women		
lonely		
happy		
foolish		
anti-social		
friendly		
bored		
artistic		

Do most people in your class have the same ideas about graffiti writers?
Do you know any graffiti writers or artists?
Is there much graffiti in your town? Where is it?

5 A good thing or a bad thing?

What do you think – is writing graffiti a good thing or a bad thing? Does everyone in your group agree?

What can we do about graffiti writers?

- Help them: put up public graffiti boards.
- Punish them: make them wash off all their graffiti.
- Don't do anything at all. It doesn't matter.
- Put up signs to stop graffiti writers.
- Other?

With one or two students, decide what to do about graffiti writers. Exchange ideas with others in the class.

17 | My beautiful dustbin

Dealing with rubbish

1 Tuning-in

What types of litter do you see most often in your town – and where?

	in buildings	*on the streets*	*in parks*	*on buses or trains*
cigarette packets				
cigarette ends				
empty bottles or cans				
sweet wrappers				
tickets				
newspapers				
other things				

Compare answers.

2 What a load of rubbish

With another student: decide what is in the bin in the picture. Make a list.

What about the bin in your classroom? Does it have the same things in it? Choose one thing from your list or from your classroom bin, and think of a new use for it. Exchange ideas.

3 Put your paper in a bin!

You are going to hear a story about some 'litterbugs' – people who throw out litter. There are these words in it:

   London   car   paper   window   laughing

With another student, try to guess what the story is about.

🔲 Now listen and be ready to retell the story.

What can we do to stop people who throw litter on to the streets? With your partner, decide which punishment is best for the people in the story:

– a weekend in prison
– a small fine
– a day picking up litter in the streets
– any others?

As a class, agree on *one* punishment.

4 The singing bin

Here are some new ideas for litter bins. Which do you like best?

- A bin that sings or plays music when you put something in it.
- A bin that says 'Thank you' each time you use it.
- A bin that has different flower perfumes when you use it.
- A bin that gives you a lottery ticket when you put something in it.
- An animal bin with a big open mouth. Its eyes light up when you use it.
- A bin that is also a street light.
- A bin that . . .

With another student, choose *two* kinds of new bin.
What colour will your bins be?
Where can you put them? Think of some good places in your town or city.

5 Unwanted words

Read the poem.

Imagine that you can throw away some English words.
With another student, talk about English words you don't like: words that
are difficult to say . . . or to spell . . . or to write . . . words with unpleasant
sounds or ideas . . .

Make a list. When you are ready, choose *one* word from your list. Make up a
short dialogue using the word.
When you are ready, say your dialogue to the class. Can they guess the
unwanted word?

At the end of the class, put all your lists of unwanted words in the bin.

18 | Up, up and away

Air balloons – advertising

1 Tuning-in

Look at the picture of an air balloon. Where did it come from? A magazine?
Is it a picture for children? Is it a design for a dress or a tee-shirt?

What do you think? Talk about the picture with the student next to you.

2 Which words go with 'balloon'?

Look at the words in the balloon below. Which words go with the idea of a balloon? With one or two other students, choose the words which go with 'balloon'.

Actions	*Things*	*Describing words*
to go up	sky	peaceful

Can you think of other words? Add them to your lists. You can use a dictionary or ask the teacher to help you.

3 Images

Simple pictures often help to sell things because they have a clear image and are easy to remember.
Look at these four images. What does each image help to sell? Talk about your ideas with other students.

Now listen to the four short advertisements. Complete the boxes.

Advertisement	Picture (A, B, C, or D)	What is it trying to sell?
1		
2		
3		
4		

Were your ideas the same as those you listened to?

4 You can sell anything with an air balloon

With another student, imagine that you both work for an advertising company. You want to use the picture of the air balloon to sell something. You can choose one of these things if you like:

wallpaper   toys   cakes   a language school
holidays   chocolates

Talk about your choice. Say why the picture can help to sell the thing you have chosen.

5 Your commercial break

You have chosen the thing you want to sell. Now think of a name for the company that sells it, for example: 'Peaceful holidays' or 'Skylight cakes'.

With your partner, write a very short television commercial for your company. Think of one or two sentences to go with the balloon picture.

When everyone is ready, present your commercial to the class. When you say the words, remember you are trying to sell something.

19 | Lifestyles

The quality of life

1 Tuning-in

You can have one of these pictures for your flat or house. Choose the one you like. Decide where to hang it and why.

With another student: talk about the room with the new picture in it.
- On which wall are you going to hang it?
- What other things are on that wall?
- What colour is the wall?
- What other things are in the room? Will the new picture go with all the other things in the room?

2 Life's simple pleasures

Do you like any of these simple pleasures?
- having a nice hot bath after work
- drinking a first cup of coffee in the morning
- phoning your parents
- playing with children
- listening to birds in the countryside
- growing plants
- going to the market
- counting your money
- sitting in the park

In small groups, talk about your simple pleasures. Think of as many as you can. Do you have time for all of them?

Now listen to three people talking about their simple pleasures. Write down the three simple pleasures as you listen:

Person 1	
Person 2	
Person 3	

Do you enjoy any of the same simple pleasures?

3 You are what you buy

Look at the pictures on the next page. Imagine that you can buy one thing from each line. Put a tick beside each choice:

	1	2	3	4
Mugs				
Cars				
Clocks				
Plants				
Musical instruments				
Books				

Sit with another student. Tell each other about your choices. Do the things you buy really show the kind of person you are?

4 The quality of life

Is the quality of life going . . . u^p↗ or d$_o$$_w$$_n$↘

In groups, talk about how the quality of life is changing.
Write down some things that show that the quality of life:

is going up   *is going down*

....

....

....

....

....

....

Where do you think these belong?

   more money   more fast food   more things in the shops
   more holidays   more police   more teachers   more newspapers
   more television channels   more cars   more motorways
   more things made of plastic

Make sure everyone in your group agrees.

5 Choices

People often have to choose between two different things.
Sit with a partner. Now look at the choices below. For each line, write down
the *one* choice you *think* your partner prefers.

I think my partner wants:
– more free time ....OR..................more money
– more new clothes ....OR..................more books
– more travel..................OR..................more new things for the home
– more time alone ....OR..................more time with other people
– more English classes..................OR..................more holidays

Tell your partner your guesses. Were you right?

20 | What did you think of this book?

Retrospective assessment of the book

1 Tuning-in

Now you have worked with this book, help us to understand what you liked, and what you did not like – and why.

With one or two students, look through the book; talk about the units you used, then decide on your three favourite units.

Write down the numbers of the units.

Try to think of reasons for your choices. Look at the reasons below. Were any of them important for you?

interesting topic   I learned interesting things.
unusual activity   I learned some useful words.
clear and easy to do   Any other reasons?
I spoke a lot of English.

Exchange ideas. Do most people in your class agree?

2 Which units did you not like very much?

Do any of these reasons explain why? Are there other reasons? In groups, compare your choices and talk about them.

uninteresting topic   too much to read before speaking
too long   too strange
not enough time   silly
too simple   ....?
too difficult

3 A speaking skills book

Imagine that you are writing another book of this kind, to help students to practise speaking English. What topics or themes are a good idea? In groups, make a list.

4 A letter to the authors

All the class together: talk about this book with your teacher. Then, in small groups, complete the following letter to the authors. Tell them your ideas about the book.

When you have finished, read your letter out to the other groups.

```
    Dear Joanne and Stephen,


        We are studying English at ....................................
in ...............................................................
We have used your book:  many times / a few times / once or twice.
We think it is ..................................................
because it .....................................................
We especially liked Unit(s) .................
because ........................................................
but Unit(s) ................. was/were not so good, because ........
................................................................
        We think ...................................
            ...................................
            ...................................
would make good topics for another book like this one.

                        Yours sincerely,
```

5 Speaking English: a progress report

Which of these statements is true for you?

– I speak English more easily now than when I began.
– I know more English but I still don't like speaking it very much.
– I'm frightened to speak because I think I will make mistakes.
– My English hasn't changed much.
– I enjoy speaking English but I still make too many mistakes.

Talk about the statements you have chosen with one or two other students. Can you help each other improve your speaking skills?

Key

Unit 1 'Sticks and stones may break my bones, but words will never hurt me' is an old English child's nursery rhyme.   1.3 Tinseltown is a name given to Hollywood.   1.5 Bomber Graham – a boxer with a strong punch; Fingers MacBride – a pickpocket; The Iron Lady – a strong and inflexible ruler; The Blonde Bombshell – a blonde actress who makes a strong impression physically.

Unit 3   3.1 Tomato red; sky blue; apple green or apple red; emerald green; wine red; olive green; raspberry red; navy blue; blood red; sea blue or sea green; bottle green; cornflower blue; cherry red.

Unit 5   5.3 The poem is by Andrew Schiller.

Unit 6   6.1 1 Saudi Arabia; 2 Liberia; 3 Sudan; 4 Malaysia; 5 Venezuela.   6.4 1 Japan; 2 Scotland; 3 Sudan; 4 USA; 5 Norway.

Unit 7   7.1 Rainbow, horseshoe, wishbone, four-leafed clover, St Christopher medal – all good luck charms.   7.2 Some of these mean good or bad luck in different countries. In England, people say 'break a leg' to an actor for good luck.

Unit 8   8.3 First recording – the dark; people ringing the doorbell or knocking at the door; water/swimming. Second recording – a hedgehog's noise, rats, water.

Unit 9   9.3 'Perfick' is an incorrect way of writing 'perfect'.

Unit 10   10.1 meat, spices, bread, preserving agents, salt.

Unit 12   12.4 The key element of the poem is that it opens up many different interpretations, suggesting the infinite variety within families. The questions are designed to stimulate discussion and have many possible answers, for example: 1 Six = Five and the speaker of the poem **or** Five = the speaker is one of the five people mentioned, e.g. a sister. 2 It could be any of the five or six. If the speaker is the father, it could mean that the three sisters are his own sisters, and so on. 3 Five ways could be: each member of the family lists the members in their own order, e.g.: Sister, sister, sister, father, mother – and so on . . .

Unit 14   14.2 Moving to a new house; getting a new job; paying a debt; a divorce settlement.

Unit 15   15.1 Recipe 1 – Irish Potato Pancakes; Recipe 2 – Playdough for children to play with; Recipe 3 – An old-fashioned mustard plaster, applied to the chest for colds; Recipe 4 – Decorated eggs (sometimes made for Easter in Northern European countries).   15.2 Recipe: ½ cup rice, 1 large onion, 3 eggs, 50 grams butter, a pinch of salt and pepper, 4 slices chicken, 125 grams mushrooms, 2 cucumbers.

Unit 16   16.1 tee-shirts, hats or shoes, words on watches or jewellery.

Unit 18   18.1 The balloon is used as a sheet to test photocopying machines.   18.3 A – a bank; B – a house removal firm; C – a firework company; D – a car.

Tapescript

Unit 2 Body shop

4 Keep fit and relax

Relax . . . Now . . . close your eyes, as tight as they'll close – squeeze them tight, tight . . . then open them gently, and relax. Now, shake your left leg from the foot right through – just shake it gently and let it relax . . . Now your right leg and your right foot. Now move your hips gently – just shake them gently on the floor . . . Now shake your shoulders gently. Now turn over on to your right side and curl your knees up to your stomach. And when you're ready, stretch out and sit up.

Unit 3 Singing the blues

6 What a wonderful world

I see trees of green,
red roses too,
I see them bloom for me and you,
And I think to myself
What a wonderful world.

I see skies of blue and clouds of white,
the bright blessed day, the dark sacred night,
and I think to myself
What a wonderful world.

The colour of the rainbow,
so pretty in the sky
are also on the faces of people going by,
I see friends shakin' hands,
sayin' 'How do you do!'
They're really sayin' 'I love you',
I hear babies cry,
I watch them grow
They'll learn much more than I'll ever know
and I think to myself
What a wonderful world.
Yes, I think to myself
What a wonderful world.

Unit 5 Opening doors

2 Where did I leave my keys?

Last summer, it was pouring with rain, as usual. So, we parked very badly in a local street. He rushed into the bank. I remembered something I had to tell him, got out of the car, locked the door, went in – and of course, when we both came to get back into the car, I'd locked the keys inside. Richard was furious – it wasted about an hour – and, ever since then, I have always carried a spare set of car keys in my handbag.

4 I turn the key

A: I turn the key, open the door, and then I put my bags down and I listen to see if I have any messages on my answerphone machine.

B: Now imagine that you have a magic key . . . and what happens . . . when you use that?

A: Well, when I use my magic key, I turn the key in the lock, I open the door, and I can smell a wonderful smell of cooking. Somebody's cooked a meal for me.

C: When I get home, I take out my key, put it into the lock, turn it and push the door. When I get into the hall, I take off my coat, hang it on a coat hook, and go into the kitchen. I put on the kettle and wait for it to boil so I can have cup of coffee.

D: O.K. . . . Today, you have a magic key . . . What happens?

C: I put the key in the lock, turn it, the door swings open, and I step into the hall. And the whole family is waiting there for me – aunts, uncles, grandparents, cousins, nephews, nieces: it's a surprise party. It's fantastic!

Unit 6 It's a small world

3 A new life in a different country
I'm thinking of emigrating to Australia. But I think that I'd really miss my friends. I think that I'd miss my family. I'd miss the English countryside. I'd miss some of the shops here because the shopkeepers are very friendly. I'd miss the taste of English food. I'd miss the house that I live in and I'd miss my family most of all.

4 International Folk Music Festival
Music from different countries – see Key.

Unit 7 Did you remember the tortoise?

3 A stroke of luck in Sweden
About ten years ago I went to visit a friend of mine . . . um . . . in Stockholm. He was an English teacher there and one day while he was at work, I went into the old part of the city to do a little shopping. There were plenty of narrow, old streets and old buildings and things and I was walking around just looking in the shop windows.

Well, there was this one window that was really . . . it was full of nice gifts: wooden things, pottery – that sort of thing. Well, this shop . . . it had a double window . . . that's . . . it had the . . . the . . . entrance door in . . . in . . . the middle between the two windows. Well, I was just looking at all the nice things in . . . in the one window, and then I moved across, past the entrance door, to look at the other window. *(pause)* Well, suddenly . . . . . . part of the top of the building . . . it just fell to the ground – bricks and stones landed right in front of the window – the . . . the . . . the *other* window – the one I had looked in about 15 seconds earlier. Yeah, well, I felt very lucky to be alive!

4 A lucky find
It was Christmas time, I was in high school, and I wanted very much to buy a beautiful dress for my high school Christmas dance. But I also needed to buy Christmas presents for my family. And I wanted to do both very much and I didn't have enough money. And I looked down in the shop, and by my foot was a $20 bill. And it solved my problem.

One day, I was in a bookshop . . . it sold very old books. I bought one and took it home. I opened the book, and found a photograph of my grandfather! It was an old photograph that my grandmother had lost many years before. She was very pleased to get it back.

Unit 8 The mad professor

3 I'm frightened of . . .
I just don't know why, but there is no way I can go to sleep at night without the light on – the bedside light. I've always been like that.

These days, I just stay where I am. I don't get out of my chair. My daughter's got a key anyway. And you hear so many terrible stories. . .

Well, I don't know what it is, but I can't do a thing about it. I just get so panicky. Everybody's tried . . . my husband, my son . . . I just can't let go of the side and I can't put my head under. I feel like screaming.

A: People are frightened of lots and lots of different things. Are you three frightened of anything in particular, any one of you?
B: Mmm. Well, I remember once being very frightened. I was alone, in the house and I heard a terrible noise coming from the garden . . . and I went out and had a look. And it was a noise, it was like . . . rrrr . . . rrrr . . . rrrr . . . it was a hedgehog! *(laughter)* They are absolutely terrifying. They make this dreadful noise.
A: What about you?
C: Ah . . . I'm terrified of rats.
A: Ah!
C: Not mice – mice don't frighten me. But rats. And . . . I'm frightened of them when they're alive, and I'm also frightened of them when they're dead!
A: What about you? Are you frightened of anything – hedgehogs, rats?
D: I'm frightened of water.
A: Water!
D: Well, when I was very young, about three or four, I fell into the canal. And of course I couldn't swim. Ah . . . and I didn't learn to swim until I was about ten or eleven. And so I've always been frightened of water.

4 You don't have to be afraid
Step 1 is to meet up with some good friends and

have a good time – have a cup of tea or something like that.

Step 2 is to arrange with your friends to go to an event with about 40 or 50 people – a fun event, like . . . a jumble sale.

Step 3 is to go with your friends again to a much larger event, perhaps a large music concert.

Step 4 is to go on your own to a similar event.

Unit 9   Once a child, always a child?

5   The missing photo

Close your eyes and listen. Think of some happy times from your childhood . . . At home, perhaps? At school? A holiday? A picnic? A party? With friends? Or family? Let some pictures of these happy times come into your head.

[*pause*]

Now choose one special time . . . a very happy time . . . imagine that you can go back and look at that special time again . . . How old are you? What are you wearing? Who is with you? Look at their clothes and faces. Are you inside or outside? Is it warm or cold? Is it daytime or evening? What can you see? What are you doing? Is it quiet? Or noisy? Are you talking about anything?

[*pause*]

You can take one photo of this special time. Who do you want in the photo? Do you want to take a secret photo? Or do you want people to look at the camera and smile? Where are they standing or sitting? When you have a clear picture, take the photo.

[*pause*]

Now come back to the classroom with your photo.

Unit 11   It's raining in my heart

3   It's raining in my heart

The sun is out
The sky is blue
There's not a cloud
To spoil the view
But it's raining
Raining in my heart.

The weatherman
Says fine today
He doesn't know

That you've gone away
And it's raining
Raining in my heart.

Oh, oh misery, oh, misery
Oh, what's going to become of me?

Unit 13   A tulip for friendship

4   A food garden

I'm going to grow carrots, because they grow fast. I'm also going to grow beetroot because I love beetroot. I also want a herb . . . rosemary perhaps. (*mm . . .*) I want to grow cucumber. And . . . lastly, I'll grow some sweet corn. Some corn on the cob . . . to make me feel warm inside. (*mm!*)

I am going to grow some potatoes . . . I'm then going to grow carrots . . . because they are very, very good for you. I'm going to grow tomatoes, because they're easy to grow and they don't need too much water, and beans, because they're full of protein. And then finally I'm going to grow some lettuce, because they are full of vitamins and lovely for salads.

Unit 14   Let's have a party

2   Let's have a party

1) Hello, Irene? Tom here. Jill and I are having a party on Friday to celebrate moving in at last, and I hope you can come – and bring a friend if you like! . . . I'd better give you the address: it's 45 Elm Street and it's . . . (*fade*)

2) Hello darling . . . Yes I got it! Get the champagne out! . . . Mm, it was really difficult. There were five of them on the panel and I was in there for hours answering questions . . . Guess what the salary is?

3) Hello, is that Lesley? It's Peter! . . . Look, I'm feeling so happy! I finally managed to pay off my Visa card – every last bit! So I thought we could celebrate by having lunch in town. Can you meet me at Harrod's? Well, yes, you see, they've got that big sale on . . . after lunch you can help me choose a new sofa and chairs for the sitting room . . .

4) Listen Mike, you must come round and have a drink now it's all over . . . I was so lucky! I got the house, the car . . . and the children, of course. He's only got his secretary . . . serves him right.

Unit 15 Ten mouthfuls of conversation

5 My recipe for . . .

Well, my recipe for a long and happy life is — well, twenty kilos of a happy family, ten ounces of good health, a great huge bunch of a loving wife, several bananas and a huge pinch of luck.

Unit 17 My beautiful dustbin

3 Put your paper in a bin!

I was driving to London once with a friend, and we suddenly saw . . . we saw someone throwing a handful of paper right out of the car in front of us. At the next red light, we stopped right beside the car. I wound down the window and shouted: 'You litterbugs! Put your paper in a bin!' Huh! They burst out laughing and drove off, throwing more and more paper and packets out of the window — laughing all the time. I was furious!

Unit 18 Up, up and away

3 Images

You won't lose any pieces if you move house with Knight's!
Go for a car that is fast, strong and exciting!
Make your money go round, at the Number One Bank!
Colourful, exciting, but safe. Buy Skyburst Fireworks for special parties.

Unit 19 Lifestyles

2 Life's simple pleasures

A: Do you have any . . . simple pleasures that you enjoy?

B: Oh . . . now, for me, one of the simplest and most pleasurable activities is making bread. (*ah* . . .) Because I love the . . . the slowness of it, and I love the feel of the dough — And I love the fact that you have to wait. The bread takes its own time. And I love the smell.

A: What about you?

C: Well, there's nothing quite like building a brick wall.

A: Oh, you're a builder!

C: Very simple. It's very straightforward. When you've built a wall and it's straight, it's one of the greatest pleasures on earth, think: I did that, and it's straight.

B: Yes . . . Yes . . .

A: Well, my simple pleasure is waking up at eight o'clock and knowing that I don't actually have to get up (*yeah* . . .) until nine-thirty (*yes* . . .) and going back to sleep. (*absolutely*) That . . . oh, it's a joy . . . bliss, bliss.

To the teacher

This book has been written to encourage the development of fluency in spoken English. It is intended for students with even elementary English language abilities. To us, developing fluency implies taking risks, letting go safely by using language in a relaxed, friendly atmosphere – an atmosphere of trust and support. Speaking fluently, of course, involves speaking easily and appropriately with others but it carries a further assumption that in simple terms says: 'What you are saying to me is more important than how accurately you are saying it'.

We have endeavoured to offer teachers and students some imaginative slants on fairly conventional and universal themes. It has been our intention to arouse curiosity and interest and also to stimulate the imagination.

Grading

The twenty units in this book are not graded linguistically and within each unit there are activities which pose varying degrees of challenge to the linguistic resources of the lower level student. Teachers, no doubt, will make their selections accordingly.

Flexibility

Each unit can be worked through in its entirety where circumstances make that an appropriate option. Alternatively, most sections within a unit can be used on their own, perhaps as an accompaniment to a coursebook unit or as a break between sessions focussing on other skills.

Personal themes

Some teachers and students may consider that some of our material has been explored in too personal a fashion. Much depends both on the type of relationship that teacher and students enjoy and also on the approach to language learning that both find comfortable psychologically. In an atmosphere of personal trust, we believe that talking about topics in personal terms strengthens and enriches the quality of social contact in the classroom. More than that, it widens the boundaries of interaction involving the target language in the future.

Involving the teacher

Students are generally interested in their teachers – their lives, their views, their attitudes. We have encouraged the involvement of teachers in the activities in this book so that they can be partners in the interaction as well as facilitators and monitors. Clearly, individual circumstances and teachers will dictate the degree to which the invitation to be involved is taken up.

The teacher as bridge

Fluency materials, especially those that explore personal themes, rely on the skill of the teacher in easing the students into the material and in setting a tone of trust and respect. It is important, in our view, for teachers to create a pathway into the units by using simple activities, mimes, visuals, or questions to elicit spoken language before opening and using the book. The book is perhaps best used after this bridge has been built and the students have thereby become oriented to the chosen unit theme or activity. What is more important is that the students should be ready to pursue the theme and keen to talk about it together. This bridging sequence is a vital part of transferring the initiative to the students and of building a positive social atmosphere. In such an atmosphere, correction becomes the servant of encouragement and precedence is given to the sharing of information, ideas and feelings.

Inexperienced teachers

Teachers who have had little teaching experience or little experience of materials like these will obviously be sensible enough to select activities and ideas from this book and adapt them to their teaching styles and to the type of classes and students they have. It is, we believe, unwise to follow the activities too closely in the hope that the book knows best. The book provides a framework only. Adapting materials is an art which teachers are expert at and we strongly encourage them to continue to develop it.

Students working together

All our units invite students to talk with one another in small groups or in pairs. Being in a classroom learning a language is essentially a social experience and should be memorable, in part, because of the relationships forged during a time of being and learning together. In fluency work one of our aims is to make learners less conscious of their vulnerability in the target language by tempting them to become interested in the people in the classroom. Risk-taking is a natural companion of such curiosity, as far as we are concerned.

Vocabulary

In some of the units we have been generous with the number of vocabulary items. This has been deliberate and reflects our belief that the strength both of the contexts and of the activities can support accelerated development of students' active and receptive vocabularies.

Cultural location

Although our material inevitably reflects our Western backgrounds, we have tried to avoid too many specific references to English-speaking locations. In several of the units we have asked students to talk about their own environments. This seems consistent with a belief that students can talk more easily and flexibly about places they know well.

The cassette

You will find the materials available on the cassette marked by 📼 in this book. The listening materials are of several types: some of the materials have accompanying comprehension tasks; other listening pieces lead the students naturally on to making spoken comparison with their own experiences; there are some music-based listening activities and finally, some of the units have recordings of people doing the speaking activities which the students themselves will eventually do. Where listening tasks have specific answers, these can be found in the key. The listening materials are intended to add variety of native speaker voice and to provide a richer base for the building of spoken fluency.

We wish you an interesting and fruitful time with the activities in this book and welcome comments and reactions from teachers who use these materials. We would also be happy to receive the letters which students write to us in Unit 20. Please send them to: Joanne Collie and Stephen Slater, c/o Cambridge University Press, The Edinburgh Building, Shaftesbury Road, Cambridge CB2 2RU, England.